Light Sensitive

A Play in Two Acts

by Jim Geoghan

A Samuel French Acting Edition

FOUNDED 1830

New York Hollywood London Toronto

SAMUELFRENCH.COM

Copyright © 1992, 1993 by Jim Geoghan

ALL RIGHTS RESERVED

CAUTION: Professionals and amateurs are hereby warned that *LIGHT SENSITIVE* is subject to a Licensing Fee. It is fully protected under the copyright laws of the United States of America, the British Commonwealth, including Canada, and all other countries of the Copyright Union. All rights, including professional, amateur, motion picture, recitation, lecturing, public reading, radio broadcasting, television and the rights of translation into foreign languages are strictly reserved. In its present form the play is dedicated to the reading public only.

The amateur live stage performance rights to *LIGHT SENSITIVE* are controlled exclusively by Samuel French, Inc., and licensing arrangements and performance licenses must be secured well in advance of presentation. PLEASE NOTE that amateur Licensing Fees are set upon application in accordance with your producing circumstances. When applying for a licensing quotation and a performance license please give us the number of performances intended, dates of production, your seating capacity and admission fee. Licensing Fees are payable one week before the opening performance of the play to Samuel French, Inc., at 45 W. 25th Street, New York, NY 10010.

Licensing Fee of the required amount must be paid whether the play is presented for charity or gain and whether or not admission is charged.

Stock licensing fees quoted upon application to Samuel French, Inc.

For all other rights than those stipulated above, apply to: Paradigm LA, 360 Park Ave South, 16th Floor, New York, NY, 10010.

Particular emphasis is laid on the question of amateur or professional readings, permission and terms for which must be secured in writing from Samuel French, Inc.

Copying from this book in whole or in part is strictly forbidden by law, and the right of performance is not transferable.

Whenever the play is produced the following notice must appear on all programs, printing and advertising for the play: "Produced by special arrangement with Samuel French, Inc."

Due authorship credit must be given on all programs, printing and advertising for the play.

ISBN 978-0-573-69485-1

**For my wife
Ruth Ann Gagen
who I took a picture of one night in
the rain.**

No one shall commit or authorize any act or omission by which the copyright of, or the right to copyright, this play may be impaired.

No one shall make any changes in this play for the purpose of production.

Publication of this play does not imply availability for performance. Both amateurs and professionals considering a production are *strongly* advised in their own interests to apply to Samuel French, Inc., for written permission before starting rehearsals, advertising, or booking a theatre.

No part of this book may be reproduced, stored in a retrieval system, or transmitted in any form, by any means, now known or yet to be invented, including mechanical, electronic, photocopying, recording, videotaping, or otherwise, without the prior written permission of the publisher.

IMPORTANT BILLING AND CREDIT REQUIREMENTS

All producers of LIGHT SENSITIVE *must* give credit to the Author of the Play in all programs distributed in connection with performances of the Play and in all instances in which the title of the Play appears for purposes of advertising, publicizing or otherwise exploiting the Play and/or a production. The name of the Author *must* also appear on a separate line, on which no other name appears, immediately following the title, and *must* appear in size of type not less than fifty percent the size of the title type.

All producers of LIGHT SENSITIVE must also provide the following billing in any publication, advertisement or production of the play, on the program's title page or on the page thereafter:

"TRIPLE EXPOSURE received its world premiere in December, 1992 at Wisdom Bridge Theatre, Chicago, Jeffrey Ortmann, Producing Director.
Under the title LIGHT SENSITIVE it received its West Coast premiere at the Old Globe Theatre, San Diego, California, Artistic Director – Jack O'Brien; Managing Director – Thomas Hall."

Light Sensitive opened at the Old Globe Theatre in December, 1992.

TOM......................................Joel Anderson

LOU...................................... Matt Landers

EDNA............................Victoria Ann-Lewis

Director: Andrew Traister
Set Designer: Nick Reid
Costume Designer: Clair Henkel
Lighting Designer: Barth Ballard
Sound Designer: Jeff Ladman
Production Stage Manager: Douglas Pagliotti

CHARACTERS

THOMAS HANRATTY, 35 to 50. Working class Irish American, lifetime resident of New York's Hell's Kitchen. Former cab driver now blind.

LOU D'MARCO, 35 to 50. Working class Italian American bartender. Funny, colorful womanizer. Not exceptionally bright.

EDNA MILES, 35 to 50. An unmarried woman from Madison Avenue. Clever, witty, resourceful and slightly lame.

Please note:
Mention is made of songs which may or may not be in the public domain. Producers of this play are hereby CAUTIONED that permission to produce this play does not include rights to use these songs in production. Producers should contact the copyright owners directly for rights and shall indemnify Samuel French, Inc. and the Author of the play against any claims arising in connection therewith.

Light Sensitive

ACT I

The LIGHTS come up one-half to reveal:

THOMAS HANRATTY sitting at his kitchen table in his tenement apartment in Hell's Kitchen. The unique feature of many of these apartments is that the bathtub is often located in the kitchen and Tom's apartment is no exception. Both TOM and his home are in a shabby state. TOM hasn't shaved or bathed in days and he probably hasn't changed his clothes either. Dishes lie dirty and unwashed, the garbage overflows, pieces of clothing lie about and a lone plant near a greasy window died long ago.

There are a number of things in Tom's apartment that seem to contrast his current state of affairs however. A fair number of black and white photos decorate the walls. These photos (Tom's) depict life on the streets of New York City unsweetened and real. They range from gritty to joyous and show more than just a little insight. A 35mm camera (circa 1975) hangs from a hook on the wall. There is also a collection of books on one shelf and, while everything else in the apartment is in disarray, these books are arranged neatly and with great care.

It is early morning, the day before Christmas Eve. TOM is drinking whiskey from a glass that once was a jelly jar. One of the reasons the kitchen is so dim is that Tom has unscrewed a light bulb from one of his few lighting *fixtures and has plugged in a record player. As we begin TOM is listening to a much-played, scratchy recording of Elvis Presley's "Here Comes Santa Claus."* HE listens for several beats when the record suddenly begins to skip. TOM stomps the floor good and hard with his foot and the record resumes playing. HE listens for several more moments. There is a KNOCK at the door.*

TOM. Yeah?
LOU. (*O.S.*) It's Lou.
TOM. It's open.
LOU. (*O.S.*) What?
TOM. It's open!

(*The door opens but the safety chain has been set. We can only see a little bit of LOU.*)

LOU. It's not open.
TOM. Huh?
LOU. You got the chain thing here.
TOM. Hold on. (*TOM silences the record player then crosses to the door. If we didn't know it yet we know it now—TOM is blind.*) Hold on. Chee. Thought I left this open. Lemme close this.
LOU. Go ahead.
TOM. Don't push.
LOU. I'm not.
TOM. Don't push. I've got to close it.
LOU. I'm not pushin'!

---

* See music note on page 6.

TOM. Watch it. Hold on. Damn shit. Hold on, hold on...
LOU. Not the latch. The chain thing.
TOM. Shut up.
LOU. The chain. The chain!
TOM. Got it. Got it. All these friggin' locks and bolts, chains and latches ... I got it.

(The door opens and LOU D'MARCO enters. LOU is near Tom's age and is bundled well against the cold. HE warms himself over a radiator.)

LOU. Jesus H. Christ it is cold this morning! Jeez! Must be ten degrees outside.
TOM. Seven.
LOU. Is that what it is?
TOM. Just heard it on the radio. Seven degrees.
LOU. Man, that's ridiculous. It's Christmas time. It never gets this cold around Christmas.
TOM. You believe it?
LOU. January, February sure. But not Christmas. I think I seen a dead guy.
TOM. Where?
LOU. In front of Smiler's. Old black geezer. I think he tried comin' in the bar a few times but I tossed him right out. He was in bad shape. You know, a bum.
TOM. Please. You mean "homeless."
LOU. Homeless, whatever. Now he's *life*less.
TOM. He really dead?
LOU. I think so. Cops was there. He wasn't movin'. They covered his head with somethin'.
TOM. Sounds like he's dead.

LOU. Mind if I turn on a few more lights?
TOM. Go ahead.

(LOU tries a wall switch, then a wall fixture. Neither seems to be working. As he does so:)

LOU. It's so dark in here I can hardly see nothin'. I could trip and break a leg or somethin'. What is this? None of your lights work?
TOM. You tell me.
LOU. You got any more bulbs?
TOM. Under the sink.

(LOU looks under the sink.)

LOU. Who keeps light bulbs under the sink?
TOM. *I* keep light bulbs under the sink! It's my house, it's where I keep them!
LOU. Well, it's a stupid place. You sure you got some?
TOM. Yeah. I saw some this morning!
LOU. You got a thing they come in but there ain't no bulbs in it.
TOM. Then I'm out. Jesus! You can see—I'm blind as a bat and I'm telling you everything!
LOU. Hold on. Wait a minute. Yeah ... *(LOU goes to the door, opens it and, while HE holds the door open with one foot, HE unscrews a light bulb in a hallway lighting fixture nearby.)*
TOM. What're you doing?
LOU. Got an idea.
TOM. What's going on?

LOU. Hold on. I'm doing somethin'. Ow! Shit, it's hot!

TOM. What are you doing?

LOU. I'm takin' a bulb from the hallway.

TOM. Great. Hey, if you get me in trouble with the landlord ...

LOU. (*Interrupts.*) Shhh ... I don't want no one to ... (*To someone down the hall.*) It's an emergency.

TOM. Who's that?

LOU. (*To other person.*) I'll replace it. I promise.

TOM. Who is it?

LOU. Some guy. Giving me dirty looks. (*To other person.*) Just for an hour or two. I swear. It's for my friend.

TOM. Is it a *fat* guy?

LOU. Yeah. (*To other person.*) It's just for a little bit.

TOM. A fat *Puerto Rican* guy?

LOU. Shhh!

TOM. (*Speaks loudly so the person down the hallway can hear him.*) You're talking to "The Scumbag"?!

LOU. Tommy ...

TOM. (*Yelling out the door.*) That sack of shit who lets his dog crap in the hallways? The guy with eight kids on welfare? You're worried about *him*? What *he* thinks of *you*?

LOU. Shut up.

TOM. Don't worry about that lazy sack of pig shit!!! He ain't sayin' nothin' to the landlord! He owes too much *rent*! That's right, pal! The whole fuckin' building knows about you! (*TOM reaches into his pocket and flings coins down the hallway.*) Here you go! Buy yourself some more crack, you fuckin' drug addict!

LOU. He's gone.

TOM. *(Still yelling.)* Hey! If I see that dog around here again I'm gonna ...

LOU. *(Interrupts.)* He's gone! C'mon, Tommy. The guy's gone.

TOM. Son of a bitch.

LOU. Jeez, you got some mouth on you.

TOM. Fuckin' hate that guy.

LOU. I heard. So did the whole building. *(LOU closes the door and screws the borrowed light bulb into a lighting fixture. LIGHTS come up to full.)*

TOM. Doesn't take his dog out. Just comes home, opens his apartment door, lets his dog go out in the hallway. Shits right in the hallway!

LOU. All right.

TOM. Know how many times I've gone down the hall to the toilet and stepped in his dog's shit?

LOU. Okay, so that happens sometimes.

TOM. That's one thing they never really come out and tell you when you go blind. They tell you this, they tell you that, but they never really come out and say it in so many words: "You're blind. You're gonna step in a lotta dog shit."

LOU. Okay, so you're pissed at the guy but you don't have to yell like that at 'im.

TOM. Yes, I do.

LOU. Why?

TOM. 'Cause he's scum.

LOU. You piss the guy off, you'll be in trouble.

TOM. Bullshit.

LOU. You don't know. You could go down the hall to the can one night and he could come at you with a knife or somethin'.

TOM. I'll kill 'im with it.

LOU. He could sneak up on you easy. Wait a minute. He wouldn't have to sneak up on you at all. He could stand right in front of you! You would *walk* right into his knife. He wouldn't have to move a muscle.

TOM. I would *smell* 'im first.

LOU. Well, it's Christmas. Peace on earth, stuff like that.

TOM. Pshew ...

LOU. I got your mail. Want to go through it?

TOM. Naw.

LOU. Might be somethin' special in here, huh? Maybe a letter from Santa.

TOM. Right.

LOU. Uh oh! An envelope with no stamp. How'd that get delivered?

TOM. Huh?

LOU. Probably 'cause the postman didn't bring it, huh?

TOM. What're you talking?

LOU. Let's take a look. See what gives. (*LOU opens the envelope.*) Uh oh! It's a Christmas card from *me*!

TOM. Pshew!

LOU. And all the guys at the Terminal Bar. Look at this. They all signed it. Kenny, Fat Freddy, George, the two Bobbys, Carmine, Roy and Howard ...

TOM. Lemme have.

(LOU hands the card to TOM. TOM holds the card close to his face feeling every bit of it with his hands. HE sniffs the card as well.)

TOM. They all signed it, huh?

LOU. Yup.
TOM. All those guys?
LOU. You bet.
TOM. The card smells like cigarettes and beer.
LOU. Well, it ain't gonna smell like flowers.
TOM. Hey, what's the card say? What's it look like?
LOU. Well, there's this chick on the cover with really big tits.
TOM. Yeah?
LOU. And she's wearin' a top, like the top of a bikini, you know?
TOM. Yeah.
LOU. But skimpy.
TOM. Right.
LOU. Real skimpy. Like you can see most of her tits burstin' out on the sides. She must be from California.
TOM. Right, right.
LOU. I mean she's got a set of bazookas on her. Madone! Man, I'd crawl over twenty miles of broken glass just to let her piss on me.
TOM. Yeah.
LOU. And inside the card it says "Merry Christmas."
TOM. All right!
LOU. You like that, eh?
TOM. Woo!
LOU. You want this card somewheres?
TOM. Yeah. On top of the fridge.

(LOU stands the card on top of the refrigerator.)

TOM. When I get a beer I can check out Miss Jingle Tits.

LOU. You wanna go through the rest of your mail? Maybe pay your gas bill?

TOM. Naw. Put it in the tub.

LOU. Yeah, well uh ... the thing is, Tom ... the tub's gettin' kinda full.

TOM. So?

LOU. So maybe you oughta take a crack at payin' some of these bills. *And* you get to take a bath. Your lifestyle improves by leaps and bounds.

TOM. Eh!

LOU. How you fixed for cash? You got cash for the holidays?

TOM. I got a little.

LOU. How much is a little?

TOM. A few bucks.

LOU. You want me to cash one of these checks?

TOM. Naw. I'll cash a check with the Chinaman.

LOU. I've got cash on me.

TOM. You got cash?

LOU. Yeah.

TOM. On you?

LOU. Five hundred bucks. Here. Here's a check for a hundred twenty-two dollars. You endorse this check and I'll deposit it in my account.

(LOU goes about the task of finding Tom's checkbook, deposit slips, opening disability checks and does all the necessary work during the following:)

TOM. How come you got so much cash on you?

LOU. I'm takin' a trip.

TOM. Yeah?

LOU. I'm goin' out of town. Almost a whole week. Right after work.

TOM. Where you going?

LOU. Vermont.

TOM. Vermont?

LOU. Yeah. Vermont. Where they make the syrup.

TOM. I know where they make the syrup! What're you going there for? There ain't nothing in Vermont.

LOU. There's trees.

TOM. Excuse me, yes, of course. How stupid of me. Yes, Lou, there are trees ... sitting in forests ... where it's colder than shit.

LOU. Yeah, but in Vermont it's a *dry* cold.

TOM. Get away!

LOU. Naw, naw, you don't feel it that much. We'll have a good time no matter what.

TOM. "We"? What "we"? Who's "we"?

LOU. Me an' Mona.

TOM. Who's Mona?

LOU. What do you mean, "Who's Mona?"! Mona. The Mona I been tellin' you about.

TOM. You haven't told me about any Mona.

LOU. Sure I did. I've been tellin' you about Mona for weeks. You just don't listen is all.

TOM. Where'd you meet her? At the bar?

LOU. Are you kiddin'? I wouldn't go out with the scuz that crawls in there.

TOM. Sorry.

LOU. Christ, you just touch any of the women comes into the Terminal Bar your cock'll fall off.

TOM. So where'd you meet her?

LOU. At school.

TOM. What school? You don't go to school.
LOU. Sure I do. See, I told you but you don't listen.
TOM. Where? Where you going to school?
LOU. It's just one course. It finished last week.
TOM. Where was this?
LOU. The New School.
TOM. That college downtown?
LOU. Yeah.
TOM. *You're* going to college?
LOU. It ain't like a real college. No one ever graduates from the New School. I just took one class. At night.
TOM. What class you take?
LOU. "Early American Cinema and Its Effect on Shaping the Racist and Sexist Values of Modern Industrial America. Part One."
TOM. Wow!
LOU. I sat in that class for twelve weeks and all I learned was the title.
TOM. Why in hell would you take a class like that?
LOU. To meet women! There was maybe a hundred people in my class. And it was loaded with women. Single women who don't look too bad yet.
TOM. You were hanging out with college women?
LOU. Yeah. Me, Lou D'Marco, talkin' cinema with college women.
TOM. Didn't they find out?
LOU. Find out what?
TOM. That you don't know nothin'.
LOU. Naw. Easiest thing to do is shut up an' listen. These college type gals love that. They live in worlds full of men who never listen to them. They meet someone like me willing to listen about their fuckin' careers and how

their biological clocks are tickin' and they go nuts. I just button up and nod a lot. When you don't talk women think you're sensitive.

TOM. Aw, they *love* that.

LOU. So you talk with some gal after class, she tells you she thinks the film had a lotta "symbolism," then you go to her place an' fuck. But first you have coffee. That's how you get to fuck college women, Tommy. You gotta have coffee with 'em.

TOM. Really?

LOU. I'm finding out the more education a woman has the less it costs to take her out.

TOM. Something's wrong with the world.

LOU. You ain't kiddin'. They ask *me* out, they want to pay the check, then they want to go to bed with me where they can't *wait* to do stuff a lot of hookers charge extra for.

TOM. Wow ... and this is how you met Mona?

LOU. Yeah. She's divorced. All these women are divorced. Get this. She's an attorney.

TOM. Phew!

LOU. Not bad, huh?

TOM. A bartender who works in the worst bar on Ninth Avenue and a lawyer.

LOU. America's an unbelievable fuckin' place, huh? See, me an' Mona, we're gonna visit her family, take walks in the snow, go antiquin' ... fresh air, sunshine. A nice change of pace. It'll do us good. You need to get out more, Tom.

TOM. I get out plenty.

LOU. Out to Smiler's, the liquor store ... You should, I dunno, just get "out" more. Go places, do things.

TOM. It's like a million below outside. Who the hell wants to go out?

LOU. It's not the point. There's such a thing as stayin' in too much. You get stale. Maybe get in a little rut or somethin'.

TOM. I'm not in a rut!

LOU. But you should be with other people. They can help you with stuff.

TOM. I don't need other people. I've got you.

LOU. (*Sneaks a pamphlet out of his pocket and tries to quote from it undetected.*) But still, when an adult is stricken with blindness, well, when that happens ... (*Reading.*) "A vast reliable network of support must be drawn upon so that the disabled individual may cope satisfactorily."

TOM. What're you reading?

LOU. Nothin'.

TOM. What're you reading?

LOU. I wasn't readin' nothin'. I swear on my mother's grave!

TOM. What've you got there?

LOU. Just this pamphlet thing here is all. I was on the east side a while back and I passed the blind place is all.

TOM. Aho!

LOU. Hey, some guy shoved this in my hand. I couldn't help it. I figured I'd read up on this blind stuff is all.

TOM. Well, keep it to yourself.

(*LOU has found a stapler. HE counts out Tom's money then folds and staples various bills.*)

LOU. Wouldn't be such a bad idea. Get somebody else in here. I mean in addition to me. Someone who could pick up some of the slack.

TOM. We don't have any slack.

LOU. Well, I dunno. Maybe in a way you do. This place don't look as clean like it used to.

TOM. Hey, I like my place the way it is.

LOU. Tom, it's a mess.

TOM. I like my place the way it is!

LOU. This place looks like a giant ashtray.

TOM. I can't see it!

LOU. But you ... now you got me confused! (*Becomes confused with the stapling of the money.*) What is it? Twenties in half?

TOM. No, twenties fold into fours, then staple.

LOU. Right.

TOM. Tens in half. Fives in half the long way. Staple at both ends. Ones are regular.

LOU. You know, blind people got their own special way of foldin' money.

TOM. So?

LOU. So they don't go around puttin' staples in their money. They teach 'em that at the blind place.

TOM. Hey, I'm doing fine, thank you. "The blind place"! You're some piece of work! You know that?

LOU. These volunteers. All they wanna do is help.

TOM. Bullshit.

LOU. Bullshit nothin'.

TOM. Bullshit!

LOU. You don't know what you're talkin'.

TOM. I know exactly what I'm talking. I know these volunteer types. I picked up plenty of them in my cab.

Plenty of them. "The Lighthouse for the Blind, driver, and please don't drive too fast. Don't smoke, driver. Slow down. Are you trying to kill us both? What's the matter with you, driver? Are you stupid? Do you speak English?" You want to know someone? Really know someone? Watch them deal with someone low. Like a cab driver. Watch how they deal with someone like that. Tells you everything. Talk to everyone like they're shit—go make nice with the blind folks. Phony, fuckin' hypocrites. I picked up plenty of them in my cab. Plenty of them. And all of them, each and every last one of them, women. Never young. Never pretty. East side women. Nothing but time and money on their hands. You getting tired of reading to me? Is it getting to be too much helping me out a little, huh? Is that it? Fuck me, is it? Fuck me, huh? (*TOM makes his way to the door.*) Uh uh. Not fuck *me*. Fuck *you*! Hear me? If this is cramping your lifestyle then take a hike, pal. Go on. Get the fuck outta here! I don't care what your fuckin' problem is, Lou. Just get the fuck out!!! (*TOM throws open the door. EDNA MILES is standing there.*) I don't need some plain, east side frump too scared and stupid to know what to do with her life come here and fuck up mine! Understand?

(*There is a pregnant silence. Finally:*)

EDNA. Hello. I ...
TOM. (*Jumps out of his skin.*) Holy shit!
EDNA. I didn't know if I should knock. I heard voices.
LOU. It's a woman from the blind place, Tom.
TOM. Aha! Yes. Yes! It all makes sense now. Yup. Fits together perfectly. Makes *perfect* sense.

LOU. (*To Edna.*) Would you just give us a minute?

EDNA. Well, I ... uh ...

LOU. Just one minute. I swear. A minute is all.

LOU. (*Closes the door leaving Edna out in the hallway.*) Listen, Tom, I didn't tell you the whole truth before because I didn't want you to get upset.

TOM. And it worked like a charm, Lou.

LOU. I ain't just goin' on a vacation to Vermont, Tom. I'm gonna be movin' there. Forever.

TOM. You're moving? To Vermont?

LOU. Yeah.

TOM. You've never even been there.

LOU. So?

TOM. So you don't even know what it's like in Vermont.

LOU. I seen calendars.

TOM. I don't believe this. Vermont's not a place you move *to*. It's a place you move *from*!

LOU. Me an' Mona, we're gonna look around. See what's up there. Jobs an' stuff.

TOM. Just like that.

LOU. Mona might be a lawyer for one of them environmental groups. The pay'd be a lot less for her but then again it's cheaper to live in Vermont. There's nothing you wanna buy. And me, well, there's lots of bars up there. There's always work for lawyers and bartenders, huh?

TOM. The two kind of go hand-in-hand.

LOU. The thing is—if I move out of the city, you'll be left with no one to ...

TOM. (*Interrupts.*) I've got people! I've got *lots* of people!

LIGHT SENSITIVE 23

LOU. No, Tom—you got no one and we both know it. You know how long it took to get this woman? Six months! That's how long ago I went down there!

TOM. Been plotting against me all along.

LOU. They got a waiting list like you wouldn't believe. This woman's a trained volunteer. She wants to help.

TOM. She can go to hell.

(There is a KNOCK at the door.)

TOM. *(Calling to door.)* Go to hell!
LOU. Shh! C'mon, she'll hear ya.
TOM. *You* go to hell. No wait. Go to *Vermont*!

(There is a KNOCK at the door again. LOU crosses and opens the door.)

EDNA. I'm sorry but it's dark out here. The light bulb is missing and it's pitch black. There's also a dog roaming the hallway ...

LOU. Yeah, come in. We were just ... You're a little early is all. We weren't expecting you.

(EDNA enters. SHE walks with a slight, almost undetectable limp. SHE also seems to have some weakness in her hand—the same side she limps on.)

EDNA. They said Saturday morning.
LOU. It's not even nine o'clock yet.
EDNA. I didn't want to be late.
LOU. What's your name?

EDNA. Edna Miles.

LOU. (*Gets his coat and readies to leave.*) Yeah, well, hi. I'm Lou. I called the blind place for my friend Tom here. He's the one who's blind. (*Sotto to Edna.*) He's a proud man. Having somebody help him is not easy for him.

EDNA. I understand. Are you going?

LOU. I'd only be in the way. Tom, this is uh ... (*LOU looks to Edna.*)

EDNA. Edna.

LOU. Edna. She's from the blind place, Tommy. She's here to read to you, help you answer your mail, go shoppin', whatever. (*To Edna.*) Right?

EDNA. Certainly.

LOU. Yeah, good. Edna, this is Thomas Hanratty. Raconteur, former kick ass stickball player and, at one time, the most dangerous white cab driver in New York City. Right, Tommy? Huh? Huh! (*No reply.*) Good luck. Hey, Tom. Merry Christmas. (*No reply.*) Merry Christmas, huh? (*No reply.*) Hey, c'mon. Merry Christmas.

TOM. Fuck you.

(*LOU shrugs to Edna, then exits. EDNA stands there not knowing quite what to say or do. Neither SHE nor TOM speaks for the longest time. Finally:*)

EDNA. So, you were a cab driver? (*No reply.*) That must have been interesting work. (*No reply.*) Driving here and there, to and fro. Picking up all kinds of interesting people. Traveling to interesting destinations. (*No reply.*) How long did you drive a taxicab, Thomas? (*No reply.*)

Perhaps I rode in your taxicab once. Wouldn't that be something? That we've already met only we don't know it. That would be interesting. Yes, very. I can remember when taxis were not just yellow. Remember? (*No reply.*) I think they had to be two tone. That was the only rule. Remember? They were blue and white, red and white, red and yellow, black and yellow ... The black and yellow taxis looked like bumble bees. I rather liked that. Didn't you? (*No reply.*) I remember being fond of black and yellow taxis. I would always hope we'd get one when Father or the doorman hailed a cab. It gave you something to look forward to ... (*No reply.*) Did you take these photos? They're quite good. Look at this one. It's beautiful. A little black girl running through an open fire hydrant. It must've been such a hot summer day. You can almost feel the water and hear her scream ... The Brooklyn Bridge ... This one's interesting. A bumpy cobblestone street. Looks like you had to lie down in the street to take it. Did you? (*No reply.*) A bag lady sleeping ... she looks so serene. These are beautiful photos. Is that Madison Avenue under all that snow? (*No reply.*) I guess driving a taxi gave you plenty of chances to take pictures. (*No reply. EDNA spies an empty beer bottle on the counter and SHE drops it into the trash. The discarded beer bottle CLINKS loudly.*)

TOM. What's that?!

EDNA. A beer bottle. It was empty. I threw it away.

TOM. Don't go doing that. Leave everything just the way it is.

EDNA. I'm sorry.

TOM. Make sounds like that. Startle me with noises every which way.

EDNA. Sorry.

TOM. Don't you know how to be around a blind person?

EDNA. I just ...

TOM. (*Interrupting.*) Wadda ya got next? A tuba?

EDNA. Sorry.

TOM. You're here like ten seconds you're already banging around the place like a maniac. I'll have a heart attack or something. Listen, Ida.

EDNA. Edna.

TOM. My friend Lou was wadda ya call it ... he acted what you might call prematurely.

EDNA. Prematurely?

TOM. You see, he thought I was in need of someone to help out because he's feeling kind of guilty he's taking off with some chick but uh, the fact is, Edna, I really don't need any help. I'm doing fine. I've got lots of people who drop by. Too many, in fact. I've got a whole network of people.

EDNA. What are you saying?

TOM. I'm saying I really don't need any help.

EDNA. From the looks of things, I'd say you need a great deal of help.

TOM. So thank you and adios.

EDNA. You want me to leave?

TOM. No! "Adios" is Spanish for "have some milk and cookies!" Yes, I want you to leave.

EDNA. But I moved things aside for this today. I made other arrangements.

TOM. So read to one of your other people.

EDNA. I don't have any other people. You're my only client.

TOM. Ho boy ...

EDNA. You're also my first.

TOM. Ug!

EDNA. On the way over here my father said reading for the blind was the stupidest idea I've ever had.

TOM. Smart man.

EDNA. He's never been right about anything. I'll be damned if he's right about *this*! You don't have a network.

TOM. She's serious!

EDNA. If you had a network, I don't think this place would look like this.

TOM. Look, lady. I don't give a crap what you think. There's been a mistake. You should never of come in the first place, understand? It's nothing personal. I just don't need any help. Okay? Thank you. Goodbye.

EDNA. No.

TOM. What?

EDNA. I said no. I'm not leaving.

TOM. You're not what?!

EDNA. I put aside these four hours and I'm going to spend them here. I don't care if we just sit here. I'll do it. I will.

TOM. Holy shit ...

EDNA. I don't care if you feel so bad for yourself that you just want to rot away. I'll stand here and watch you rot. At least you won't rot alone. I'm not going. For all I care we can both stay here in stone silence listening to the sound of your insides getting hard and crusty.

TOM. You're not going to go?

EDNA. That's right.

TOM. I've asked you to leave but you're not going to.

EDNA. Correct.

TOM. (*Flabbergasted.*) This is ... it's ... I can't believe you would ... Hey! All right, all right. Enough, sister. Scram. Get your ass out of here!

EDNA. I'm not leaving.

TOM. Hey, enough! Get out!

EDNA. No.

TOM. Get out!

EDNA. I said no.

TOM. (*Screaming.*) GET OUT!!! How could you ... I said GET OUT!!! GET ... OUT!!! (*No reply.*) I could toss you out of here. I hope you know that, lady. I could eject you *physically*.

EDNA. Perhaps.

TOM. No "perhaps" about it! I've lived thirty years in this apartment. I know every square inch. I'd have you in a corner in no time and out the door five seconds after that.

EDNA. Like I said ... perhaps.

TOM. Please just go and the whole thing'll be forgotten.

EDNA. Uh-uh.

TOM. Look, it's not your fault. It's nothing personal against you, Edna. There was just a mix-up ... a misunderstanding. Lou thought I might need some help—it turns out I don't. Thank you very much, but I won't be needing you. Goodbye.

EDNA. No.

TOM. Hey, c'mon. I want you out of here.

EDNA. No.

TOM. Get out.

EDNA. No.

TOM. Get out!

EDNA. No!

TOM. Get out, Goddamn it!!! I said get out!!! (*No reply.*) Do a thing like this to me? My own home?!

(TOM begins to slowly circle the table as EDNA keeps her distance.)

TOM. This is my home, understand? I want someone out—they're out.
EDNA. Go ahead. Just try and catch me.
TOM. You're out of here ...
EDNA. Not so. I'm like a jungle cat. I can move like you wouldn't believe. I'll just skip and twirl my way around this room. Zip! Twirl!

(TOM makes a sudden grab for Edna and stumbles. His hand comes to rest upon a broom. HE breaks off the bristle end of the broom with astonishing ease, then brandishes the stick.)

TOM. Okay, fine ... Let's see you zip your way around this.
EDNA. What are you doing?
TOM. Real smart ass, aren't you? (*Mocking her.*) "I'm not going." We'll see about that.
EDNA. You're not going to hit me with that, are you?
TOM. It's up to you, babe.
EDNA. You wouldn't.
TOM. A man has the right to choose who stays in his own home.
EDNA. Put that down.
TOM. No.
EDNA. Put that down!!!

TOM. (*Mocking her.*) No!!!
EDNA. You swing that at me ...
TOM. Uh huh.
EDNA. You just swing that at me ...
TOM. Oh, I'm going to swing it at you all right ...
EDNA. You do and I'll ... I'll ...
TOM. You'll what?
EDNA. I'll ... (*Thinks—then.*) I'll shoot you.
TOM. What?!
EDNA. I'll shoot you. I've got a gun. And, believe me, I know how to use it. (*EDNA opens her purse, then snaps it shut.*) There, it's out. If you do anything that looks like an act of violence against me—so help me God—I'll drop you like a rock.
TOM. A gun ...
EDNA. That's right. I don't want to use it but if I have to I will.
TOM. And what kind of gun is this, if I might ask?
EDNA. A silver one.
TOM. A silver one. Sounds dangerous.
EDNA. It does the job.
TOM. You carry a gun?
EDNA. This is New York. Doesn't everyone?
TOM. You don't have no gun.
EDNA. Think so?
TOM. Yeah.
EDNA. Pretty sure of yourself, aren't you?
TOM. East side lady from the Lighthouse don't carry no gun.
EDNA. Not even one who was mugged? ... and told herself "Never again. No one does that to me again ... *ever!*"

TOM. You're lyin'.
EDNA. You're positive?
TOM. Total bull.
EDNA. Then go ahead. Take a swing. (*EDNA crosses nearer to Tom and stands before him.*) If you're so sure about your ability to know a complete stranger you can't even see ... then knock my block off. Go on. (*EDNA silently picks up an empty beer bottle and holds the top end against Tom's forehead.*) I'll put a bullet right in your thick head. Maybe it'll knock some sense into you.

(*TOM and EDNA stay like this for the longest time as Tom tries to figure out if Edna is bluffing or not. HE finally lowers his broom handle.*)

TOM. I need a drink. (*TOM pours from his scotch bottle but it's empty.*)
EDNA. It's empty ...
TOM. I can tell that!!! (*TOM crosses to a cupboard and takes out a gift wrapped bottle of scotch. HE unwraps it quickly and pours himself some.*)
EDNA. Gift wrapped. Someone give you scotch for Christmas?
TOM. No, I was going to give it to Lou, but ... (*Catches himself.*) What am I doing talking to you?! I don't want you here—you're not here!
EDNA. Lord, you're thick ...
TOM. *I'm* thick. You're waving a loaded gun around and *I'm* thick. Look, lady. Here it is plain and simple. As of this very moment, you are not even here.
EDNA. I see.

TOM. I tried to deal with you rationally, but it didn't work. So you want to stay—stay. But you're not here. I'm going to go about my business like I always do. As if you're not even in this room.

EDNA. Do as you wish.

TOM. I will. You've got the dullest four hours of your life coming up.

EDNA. You've obviously never been to the opera.

TOM. Huh?

EDNA. Nothing.

TOM. I don't even know what I'm talking to you for. You're not here! I'm going about my day like I'm alone. You're blocked out completely. I'm just going to have my normal routine like I always do. (*Struck by a thought.*) In fact, about this time every day, I take my bath. Yeah. That's what I do. I take my bath about this time every day.

EDNA. It looks like you skipped a few months.

TOM. (*Begins to clean the mail out of his bathtub.*) Climb in there, take a nice, long, hot bath. That's what I'm going to do. Fill up the tub, strip down and hop in.

EDNA. That's my favorite part.

TOM. Somebody say something?

EDNA. Definitely. The strip down part. It's my favorite. I'm a big fan of the male anatomy. You bet I am.

TOM. Uh huh.

EDNA. Those male strip clubs like Chippendale's and such, I go all the time. Nothing I like better than to see a tight pair of buns hanging out of a satin g-string. Just peel slowly, will you, Tommy? And save the socks for last, okay? I've got a thing for feet. Oh, gee. I just realized. You're going "all the way." This'll be even better than Chippendale's. I'll get to see *everything*. Can you give me a sneak preview? Wadda ya say, huh? Whip that puppy out. C'mon, let's take a peek at Tommy Junior.

TOM. You're some twisted piece of work, lady. Are you serious?

EDNA. I am if you are.

TOM. You're crazy. I'm sitting in my kitchen with a sex pervert with a gun!

(TOM has abandoned his bathtub bluff by now. EDNA crosses to the kitchen sink where SHE washes a glass, dries it and eventually helps herself to some of Tom's scotch.)

EDNA. I was just thinking.

TOM. Of what?

EDNA. My father's probably going to ask me how this went.

TOM. Just tell him the truth. You teased and tormented a blind man on the day before Christmas Eve.

EDNA. Have you been blind for long, Thomas?

TOM. You're still not going?

EDNA. Not only am I not going—I'm going to drink some of your scotch.

TOM. (*Pushes the bottle to the other side of the table.*) Please. I insist. Take the *furniture* with you while you're at it!

EDNA. Have you been blind for long? (*No reply.*) Have you been blind for long? (*No reply.*) It's called conversation. You have the advantage. You can picture anyone you'd like. You like Oriental hookers? Well, I'm poured into a black satin dress split clean up the side. I'm wearing black fingernail polish and a ring on each finger.

(*Like an Oriental hooker.*) "So, American big boy ... You like Ting Lu? You been blind for long?"

TOM. Eight years.

EDNA. How did it happen?

TOM. The way I went blind?

EDNA. Yes.

TOM. Don't you have all that in your handy little file from the Lighthouse?

EDNA. Sure, but it's so much more delicious when I hear it first hand.

TOM. If I tell you, will you go?

EDNA. Okay.

TOM. You will?

EDNA. Why not? All I want is a tragic story to share with the girls at tea—then I'm gone.

TOM. Okay. Deal. Come this February it'll be eight years. I'm at the bar with Lou one night and it's cold, real cold, as cold as it is today, maybe even colder. It's four in the morning. Lou's closed the bar. He's got the door locked, we're inside drinkin'. We're doing some *serious* drinking. *Very* serious drinking. We're shitface is what we are.

EDNA. Yes.

TOM. Time to go home, I walk with Lou out to his motorcycle. His cycle has been sitting in sub-zero weather for twelve hours and the battery is dead. I've got my cab, there's a pair of jumper cables in the trunk. Lou says, "Gimme a jump start." I don't want to. I tell him he's too drunk to ride a motorcycle over the Fifty-ninth Street Bridge in two degree weather, he tells me I'm too drunk to drive a cab, I tell him to go to Hell, we have a fist fight. There we are, two drunks on Ninth Avenue at four in the morning beating the crap out of each other to see who's more sober. Lou wins the fight, so I agree to give him a jump start. Is a taxicab battery the same voltage as a motorcycle battery? Can you *do* such a thing? We don't know. We're drunk out of our minds! I hook up the cables to his battery, take the other end over to the cab's battery, touch the terminals and my battery explodes in my face. I've got battery acid everywhere. My face, my hands, I can taste it in my mouth, my eyes ... I'm in shock. I'm running around. Lou's trying to catch me. We're drunk, we're falling down. There's traffic coming down Ninth Avenue. I try and stop a car ... I'm waving my arms. "Help me! Help me! God! Help me!" Who's going to stop on Ninth Avenue at four in the morning for someone yelling "Help me!"? Huh? Would you? (*No reply.*) By the time I got to the hospital both my corneas had been too damaged for them to ... I can't even see silhouettes or blurs or shapes. Just black.

EDNA. I'm sorry.

(*There is a silence. By now very little of Tom's apartment has escaped Edna's eye.*)

EDNA. You don't seem to be big on food.
TOM. Huh?
EDNA. Your kitchen. There's not much to eat.
TOM. Yeah, well, I usually just pop out to Smiler's and ... Hey, weren't you going to leave?
EDNA. (*Examining can.*) You paid two dollars and fifteen cents for a can of chili?
TOM. I said, weren't you going to leave?
EDNA. Is that what they charge?

TOM. You said you were going to go.
EDNA. I lied. Is this what they charge?
TOM. Yes! That's what they get at Smilers! If it *says* two dollars and fifteen cents then I *paid* two dollars and fifteen cents! Now, you said you would ...
EDNA. (*Interrupting.*) A dollar five in New Jersey.
TOM. You live in New Jersey?
EDNA. No, Eighty-fifth and Madison.
TOM. Excuse me!
EDNA. But my father drives me out to Newark once a week, sometimes twice. We load up on everything. It's *so* much cheaper out there it's ridiculous. Know what I could do?
TOM. What? Pick up a few items for me? Do my shopping *for* me?
EDNA. No, that would be a lot of extra work that I'm not willing to do.
TOM. Oh ...
EDNA. What I was about to suggest was you come with us. My father takes the Lincoln Tunnel. We drive right by this building. You could do your weekly shopping and save a lot of money. Do you want to do that?
TOM. Well, uh ... there's all kinds of stores on Ninth Avenue, you know. I mean besides Smiler's. There's, uh, well, you know, there's a Puerto Rican deli on Forty-fifth, and uh the Korean grocery store ... you know ... cheese and milk ... fruit ... stuff ...
EDNA. Is that a "yes" or a "no"?
TOM. Your old man's got a car?
EDNA. Yes. It's his hobby.
TOM. Hobby?

EDNA. Yes. When Daddy retired, he read an article about men who stop working without making plans. The article claimed men who don't plan for their retirement have a life expectancy of only a few years.

TOM. So?

EDNA. So that was my father. He read the article and got scared. Very scared. One day he asked my mother and me to come outside. There, parked at the curb, was this car. A Chevrolet. A four door, black Chevrolet. The most unimaginative car I'd ever seen. I had no idea a car could come with so little chrome! He parks it on the street. We live in the most competitive parking environment in the world and my father's plan to stay involved with life is to battle for parking spots with this drab automobile. Moving the car once a day would be enough aggravation for anyone, but my father *thrives* on it. He'll see someone putting on their coat and he's on them like a hawk. "Going somewhere? Need a lift?" "No," we tell him. "Don't give up your parking space. You worked so hard for it." It means nothing to him! He gives up a parking space he got up at six a.m. to get just to drive you to somewhere where he can circle the block and wait for you so he can drive you back home and circle the block again looking for another parking spot. He's out there right now. Circling the block. Like a shark. Waiting for me to fail. He's not playing the radio because the car doesn't *have* one. They wanted ninety dollars extra for a radio. So he's circling the block. Silently. Windows fogging up. Round and round.

TOM. This is his retirement?

EDNA. I'm afraid so.

TOM. That's crazy. Now, you take my father. When he retired, he did it right. He retired on a Friday, hung around the house Saturday and Sunday, come Monday, he went to the Terminal Bar and he went there every morning like clock-work for three months. Religiously. That's how I met Lou. The guy you met. Lou works at the Terminal Bar.

EDNA. The "Terminal Bar"?

TOM. Yeah. It's next to the Port Authority Bus Terminal.

EDNA. Oh.

TOM. Yeah. So my old man'd get so wasted, there wasn't no way he could make it home. Lou would call me, say "Come and get your old man." I'd hop down to the Terminal Bar and get him. Lou and I became friends. At least, we were.

EDNA. What happened?

TOM. To me and Lou?

EDNA. No, to your father.

TOM. He died. Right at the bar. One minute he was talking to some guy—next minute he was stone cold dead.

EDNA. How ironic.

TOM. What?

EDNA. Your father. He died at the Terminal Bar.

TOM. Huh?

EDNA. "Terminal." He died at the ...

TOM. (*Getting it.*) Oh! Right. Yeah. I never thought of it that way. Right. "Terminal." They keep a shot glass with some whiskey in it on a shelf above the cash register. Sorta like a tribute. There's five or six glasses up there. All the guys who died at the bar over the years.

EDNA. (*Offering toast.*) To your father.

TOM. Huh?

EDNA. I'm making a toast to your father.

TOM. Sure, why not.

(THEY drink.)

EDNA. What was he like?

TOM. What was he like ... Well, you'd like my father. Everyone did. Liking him was probably the easiest thing a person could ever do. He was the most beloved man in this neighborhood. If they were electing a mayor of Ninth Avenue, he would've won by a landslide. The man's middle name was charm. He had buckets of it. On the street, he was the nicest man you could ever know. To walk with him was like walking with a celebrity or something. I used to wait for him at the bus stop on 42nd Street every night just so I could walk home with him. So I could be seen with him. He was so well liked. On the street. And only on the street. Because at home he was the coldest, most ruthless, black-hearted son-of-a-bitch that ever brought home a paycheck. He spent his time in this apartment like he was serving a prison sentence. This silent, smoldering mountain of a man that you were too afraid to even talk to. He beat me. Beat me so bad I joined the Army the minute they'd take me. Beat my sister. Christ, he beat my mother like a dog. See the doorway?

EDNA. Yes.

TOM. There used to be a door there. A French door. With all the panes of glass.

EDNA. No ...

TOM. Pushed me through it when I was sixteen. I came at him with a heavy frying pan and he threw me right through the French door. Took forty-eight stitches at Saint Clair's emergency room. Somewhere along the way, between the time my father met my mother and the day he died, somewhere in that space of time someone did something that put a bug up his ass. A great, big, black, creepy-crawly bug got up his ass one day and stayed there. And we, my mother, my sister and me, we were supposed to guess how to get the bug out. With every little thing we did, every single move we made. My mother ... I felt the worst for her. Married to a man that has every heart in the neighborhood in his pocket—he comes home and he doesn't even bother to say hello. Silence. Not so much as a grunt to acknowledge she *exists*. Just another day of punishing her for something ... Sometimes I have this awful thought about the man. Sometimes I think my father was warm and friendly with everyone just so it would hurt my mother all the more. And if that's true, then why was my father not the cruelest, most heartless person who ever existed?

EDNA. Because my father is.

TOM. No way.

EDNA. I'm serious.

TOM. No one was worse than my father.

EDNA. My father would go to the office in the morning and ruin the life of someone like your father just for *practice*.

TOM. That doesn't count. That's just business.

EDNA. My father is the most heartless, loveless man who ever lived. I'm sure your father was bad, too, but he'll have to take second place.

TOM. For cruelty and not loving—my father takes second place to *no one*.

EDNA. He does this time.

TOM. Uh uh.

EDNA. Oh, yes.
TOM. Sorry.
EDNA. *I'm* sorry.
TOM. Get away.
EDNA. I can prove it.
TOM. Baloney.
EDNA. I can. I can tell you a story about my father—it wouldn't even have to be his worst story—I could tell you about him and you would have no choice but to say, "Yes, you're correct. Your father *is* the most heartless man who ever lived."
TOM. Never.
EDNA. Want to bet?
TOM. Sure. What're we betting?
EDNA. If I lose—I go. Get my coat, walk out the door, I'm gone. I win—I stay. I mean, I get to come back.
TOM. I dunno.
EDNA. You get to judge.
TOM. How do you know I won't say you lose just so you'll go?
EDNA. Because you'd have to lie and that would mean you have no soul, like my father, and I could never read to a man with no soul.
TOM. All right. Go 'head.
EDNA. Very well.
TOM. But I'm warning you, if I feel in my heart your father's not any worse ... you're gone.
EDNA. Fair enough.
TOM. Go 'head. Shoot.
EDNA. Give me a minute. Let me think. (*EDNA helps herself to some more scotch as SHE thinks. Finally:*) I'm just thinking ...

TOM. Take your time.

EDNA. There are so many tales to choose from. Here, this will do. It's short, yet numbing. We rented a house in the woods one summer. I was twelve. We had never spent any time in the country to speak of. A visit here, a half day there. This would be an entire month and I can't tell you how I was looking forward to it. Our first night in the country, and I was just about to fall asleep when I heard this terrible racket. I got up, looked out my window and there they were. A family of raccoons going through our metal trash cans! I was thrilled beyond words! Live animals, cute ones, no less, at our back porch pawing through our garbage. I watched from my window and simply ... *giggled.* My welcoming committee were these bandits complete with masks and they made all this entertainment from refuse. The next night I couldn't even *think* about sleeping. I put a pillow on my window sill and waited for the raccoons. I remember one of them had a fondness for orange rinds and I had left some at the top of our garbage for him. I fell asleep waiting. An hour or two must've gone by when suddenly the trash cans rattled. I woke up instantly. The raccoons were back. The biggest one—he must have been a male—the leader—he was on top of a trash can trying to get to the orange rinds when someone ... There was a shot. This gunshot rang out and he fell backward off the trash can six or eight feet from the force of the bullet onto his back. He flailed his arms and legs in the air for just a moment or two and then he was dead.

TOM. And your father shot the raccoon. Listen, I'm sorry, but that's not ...

EDNA. (*Interrupting.*) Apparently you can shoot a raccoon who goes through your garbage, but there's no guarantee the others will stay away. Not unless you do what my father did. Yes, my father shot the poor animal. He stepped out from behind some bushes where he had waited for the raccoons like some great white hunter. This was my father's first official act with nature. To kill something. He had a rope with him. And he tied the rope around the dead animal's hind legs then dragged him out to the edge of the woods and hung him from a tree. Not high. Just a few feet. The other raccoons who had run away— they came back to the edge of the woods to the tree. They gathered around their dead friend in a circle and mourned him with a grief I did not know existed. They stood in a perfect circle and wailed these shrill cries of anguish until I thought I would go insane from their misery. They flung themselves upon the ground, held and comforted each other and looked to our house as if to say, "Are you *insane*? Why? Why!" And when they were done they moped off into the woods. We rented that house for the next three summers. The raccoons never came back. My father brags about that to this day. How he protected our coffee grinds and egg shells one night in July.

(EDNA has clearly won her wager with Tom. HE goes to speak but stops himself. HE tries again, then stops. Finally:)

TOM. You really wearing a black dress with a slit?
EDNA. Am I what?
TOM. You know what you said before? The Oriental gal and the dress ...

EDNA. Oh. No, I'm not.

TOM. Just thought I'd ask.

EDNA. Did you take these photos?

TOM. Yes. Years ago.

EDNA. They're wonderful.

TOM. Thank you. See the camera hanging on the wall? Guy got in my cab and left it in the back seat.

EDNA. Oh my ...

TOM. I dropped him off at Grand Central. So much for finding him there. The cab company had a lost and found department: my boss's *living room*! So I kept the camera.

EDNA. Wise choice.

TOM. That's how I got into photography. Someone left a camera in my taxi. You work, Edna?

EDNA. At home, yes. I don't have a regular job as such, but there's so much that needs doing. I nursed my grandfather when he died several years ago. Then my grandmother. People said she would go right after him.

TOM. That happens a lot, yeah.

EDNA. I got to go to Washington last summer. Turns out a grand aunt was dying. I got to see the Washington Monument on the way to the cemetery.

TOM. Oh.

EDNA. My brother Andrew. He died young. I nursed him. Mother is not well. I'm sure she'll be next. I'll nurse her. Then Father will die. Then my work will be done.

TOM. Well, it's nice to have things planned.

EDNA. Not very Christmassy conversation, I suppose.

TOM. It's okay. Christmas seems to treat some people better than others. I've always liked Christmas, but somehow Christmas Eve, Christmas Day ... I always seemed to be driving a cab. Midtown has no traffic, everyone wants a cab, tips are great. You get what you can out of Christmas.

EDNA. Yes. Is there any last minute shopping you'd like to do? I have time still.

TOM. Naw, not really.

EDNA. Gift wrapping, Scotch tape, ribbon? We could go get some.

TOM. My gift list was just Lou this year. I got him a lovely bottle of something which we're drinking right now.

EDNA. (*Offering toast.*) To Lou.

TOM. To Lou.

(THEY drink.)

TOM. I went to Saint Patrick's Cathedral for midnight mass last Christmas. Man, I figured that oughta be something. The choir, the organ, the smell of incense ... But I get there and they tell me I need *tickets*. Tickets! They turn me away from midnight mass because I don't have a *ticket*!

EDNA. A lot of people want to go.

TOM. Seems that way.

EDNA. It's like a Broadway musical.

TOM. I'll bet.

EDNA. I have tickets.

TOM. To what?

EDNA. Saint Patrick's, tomorrow night, midnight mass.

TOM. How'd you get them?

EDNA. My father is a big contributor to Saint Patrick's. I have two tickets. Would you like to go?

TOM. You won't need the other ticket?
EDNA. No.
TOM. No one else you want to take?
EDNA. No.
TOM. What about your father?
EDNA. His sister is arriving at Newark at eleven at night and he insisted on picking her up.
TOM. Well, Jeez, midnight mass at Saint Patrick's. Sounds mighty tempting. Yeah, sure. I'll go. Yeah, what the Hell. Let's do it.
EDNA. Shall I come by here first?
TOM. Sounds like a plan. Say eleven o'clock?
EDNA. Could we make it ten-thirty? I'd like to get there early.
TOM. Fine.
EDNA. I'd like to light a candle for my brother Andrew.
TOM. I'll light one for my mother.
EDNA. Then we can say a prayer if you'd like. A prayer to Saint Odilia.
TOM. She a patron saint?
EDNA. Yes.
TOM. For who?
EDNA. The blind and hopeless causes.
TOM. I had to ask. Listen, Edna, can I ask you a question?
EDNA. Sure.
TOM. Tell me the truth. No bull.
EDNA. All right.
TOM. Did you really have a gun before?
EDNA. Well, if you must know ... (*EDNA is about to tell Tom the truth but thinks better of it.*) Yes ... but I was only going to shoot you in the leg. (*EDNA exits. Finally:*)
TOM. Oh ...

(*The LIGHTS fade to BLACK.*)

ACT II

It is exactly eight days later—New Year's Eve morning. Tom's apartment is much improved. Clothes no longer lie about, the floor is shiny clean, the garbage no longer overflows, there are no dirty dishes in evidence, things are neat, orderly and pleasant looking. Tom's cupboard is fully stocked with neatly arranged groceries. The formerly greasy window is now clean and it even sports a frilly curtain. The dead plant is gone and in its place there is a live, healthy plant.

As we begin the stage is empty. From outside we can hear the occasional faint sounds of New Year's eve PARTY HORNS. The hot water kettle on the stove begins to whistle. TOM hurriedly enters from his bedroom. HE is just finishing getting dressed. TOM's appearance is much improved, too. HE looks neat and clean shaven, and his clothes are freshly washed and pressed, although not much can be said for his color selection. TOM goes about the task of making a pot of tea. When HE is just about done there is a KNOCK at the door.

TOM. Who is it?
EDNA. (*O.S.*) It's me.
TOM. Just a second. (*TOM disappears into his bedroom for a moment then returns with a sweater in a bizarre color or pattern. HE quickly puts it on, pats his hair, etc. and goes to speak. HE stops himself. HE sits at his kitchen table and strikes a nonchalant pose.*) It's open.

EDNA. (*Tries to open the door but the chain has been set.*) Tom?
TOM. Huh?
EDNA. The chain is on.
TOM. The what?
EDNA. The chain, Tom. I can't open the door.
TOM. Oh! Wait. Hold on. Lemme get that. Hold it. Just one sec. (*TOM crosses to the door and unlatches the chain easily.*)
EDNA. Sorry.
TOM. Uh uh. Not your fault. I'm always putting this thing on and forgetting about it. There.

(*EDNA enters. EDNA's appearance has changed somewhat, too. SHE has had her hair done, SHE's wearing makeup and SHE also wears a dress that looks closer to spring than winter.*)

EDNA. Hello.
TOM. Hi. I'm sorry about the door.
EDNA. It's all right.
TOM. I'm always putting up the chain then telling people, "It's open!" (*Laughs nervously.*) Heh heh ... It used to drive Lou nuts. "The chain! The chain!" Well, you just saw ...
EDNA. In a city like New York, it's best to keep your door locked in the first place.
TOM. You're right. All kinds of creeps and weirdos crawling around.
EDNA. Yes.
TOM. Yes.
EDNA. Well ...

TOM. Yeah.
EDNA. Sorry I'm late.
TOM. Were you late? I didn't even know.
EDNA. There are people starting to celebrate New Year's Eve already. It's not even noon.
TOM. Can you believe it?
EDNA. The police had some streets closed off of Times Square. My cab driver had to take a detour.
TOM. Aha.
EDNA. Well.
TOM. Well. (*Then:*) I made some tea.
EDNA. Really?
TOM. Actually I'm *making* tea. Just poured the water. It'll be ready in a minute.
EDNA. Oh, good. I'd love some.
TOM. You got it.

(THEY both laugh nervously.)

TOM. It's your favorite, too. English Breakfast tea.
EDNA. Oh, how nice.
TOM. Even though it's nowhere near breakfast.

(THEY both laugh nervously.)

EDNA. And we're nowhere near England.
TOM. Huh?
EDNA. English Breakfast tea. We're nowhere near England.
TOM. (*Getting it.*) Oh! Yeah! Right!

(THEY both laugh nervously, then.)

TOM. Funny.
EDNA. Hmm ...
TOM. Hmm ...
EDNA. Don't you look nice.
TOM. Aw, this? This is just knock around stuff I wear. Like the sweater?
EDNA. It's interesting.
TOM. Nice, huh?
EDNA. *Very* interesting.
TOM. Knew you'd like it. I've had it for a while.
EDNA. You bought it when you could see?
TOM. No.
EDNA. Aha.
TOM. But it was a few years ago. I went down to Canal Street. Old geezer who runs the store says, "What're you lookin' for?" I tell him I need a sweater. He says, "What kind of sweater?" Can you imagine that? He took the time to ask me what *kind* of sweater I was looking for. I say, "I'm looking for a classic Christmas sweater. One that's red mostly and white with a picture on it that looks like it was done in needlepoint. You know, Santa, his sled, people ice skating, like that ..." He says, "You're in luck. I just got one of those in today." And he sells me this one.

(Tom's sweater is nothing like his description.)

EDNA. It's lovely.
TOM. I haven't worn it that much. But this seemed like the time to take it out. My corny Christmas sweater. Tea must be ready by now.
EDNA. Would you like me to ...?

TOM. Uh uh. Let me. You sit. Relax. (*TOM goes about the task of serving Edna tea.*)
EDNA. Guess what I just saw outside.
TOM. A dead guy?
EDNA. God no. Why on earth would you guess that?
TOM. In this neighborhood it's not that wild a guess.
EDNA. Well, it wasn't a dead person.
TOM. I give up.
EDNA. I saw a white cat. Right outside, in front of the building. He was beautiful ... sleeping on a pile of plastic garbage bags. Pure, snow white. Not the slightest smudge on him.
TOM. A pure white cat in this neighborhood?
EDNA. Yes.
TOM. Must've fallen off a truck from Jersey.
EDNA. There's going to be a miracle.
TOM. Hmm?
EDNA. When you see a pure white animal, that means there's going to be a miracle. That's what Sister Mary Sebastian used to tell us. "Before God performs one of his miracles, he sends down an angel in the form of a white animal. To make sure His miracle goes the way He wants it."
TOM. Who told you that?
EDNA. Sister Mary Sebastian. Fifth grade.
TOM. And where did she come up with that?
EDNA. No idea.
TOM. "There's going to be a miracle." That's rich. How old was Sister Mary what's-her-name?
EDNA. Sebastian.
TOM. How old was she?
EDNA. At the time—in her eighties.

TOM. Well, that's what eighty years of no sex will do. You start making up stories about white cats and miracles.

EDNA. No, this is going to happen. I can feel it in my bones the way you feel the cold sometimes. I've been feeling this way ever since we prayed together in Saint Patrick's. Something really wonderful is going to happen and it's going to happen right here. The cat, it looked at me as if to say, "Don't look so surprised. You know why I'm here. I'm here for the miracle."

TOM. Edna, this neighborhood, Hell's Kitchen, it wasn't built for miracles. It was built for tragedy. That's why all the apartments are too small. So people can bake in the heat of summer, get drunk and kill each other. I've lived here my entire life. The only miracle I've ever seen is when my father left something in the bottle.

EDNA. You just wait. Wait 'til something good happens and you were the only one who didn't believe it was coming.

TOM. If that happens I will personally apologize, buy you lunch, then give the white cat a blow dry. (*TOM offers to pour some whiskey in Edna's tea.*) Want some?

EDNA. No, I shouldn't.

TOM. It's like Irish coffee except you do it with tea.

EDNA. No.

TOM. I make lousy tea. It'll kill the taste.

EDNA. I don't think so.

TOM. I hate to drink alone.

EDNA. No thanks.

TOM. You sure?

EDNA. I'm sure.

TOM. Just one?

EDNA. No.

TOM. It's New Year's Eve.
EDNA. Okay.

(TOM pours whiskey in both of their teas.)

EDNA. Guess where I went yesterday.
TOM. No idea.
EDNA. The New School.
TOM. *(Chokes on his tea.)* The wha ...?
EDNA. Are you all right?
TOM. I'm fine, I'm fine ... What's this about the New School?
EDNA. It's where I registered to take a class. It's one night a week.
TOM. Ooo, Edna. Edna, Edna, Edna ... Don't you know about that place?
EDNA. Know about what?
TOM. What goes on over there? What kind of people go there?
EDNA. What are you talking about?
TOM. There are a lot of—how can I put this in a nice way—there are a lot of real smooth, smarmy guys on the make over there who are looking for only one thing and it ain't no education.
EDNA. Where did you hear this?
TOM. It's something everybody knows.
EDNA. *I* never heard any such thing.
TOM. Then I'm surprised. Because it's a basic, well known fact about New York City. New York City: it's cold in the winter, the subways smell of urine and the New School's got a lotta horny gigolos in it.

EDNA. Well, I'll just have to be extra careful in my Tuesday night Shakespeare class.

TOM. You do that. I'm not kidding, Edna. That place is like a shark tank. Watch yourself.

EDNA. I will.

TOM. You're taking Shakespeare, huh?

EDNA. To start.

TOM. They cover any of his sonnets?

EDNA. Some. And about six of his plays.

TOM. Maybe we could read some of his stuff one of these days, huh?

EDNA. I'd love to. You like Shakespeare?

TOM. Love 'im! I've read all his plays. Some of them more than once. And those romantic poets. You know, the British guys.

EDNA. Shelley, Byron ...

TOM. Yeah. I'm nuts for that stuff. In high school, Mister Kaiser made everyone memorize twenty lines of a sonnet by a romantic poet for an exam. Man, guys were forcing that stuff into their brains like it was poison. Me? I had twenty lines memorized in no time. I aced the exam and a few of the guys got suspicious. Thought I actually *liked* poetry.

EDNA. Uh oh.

TOM. You'd better believe it. You don't want to go through high school in New York City known as a "lover of poetry" believe me. It's easier to be known as a drug addict.

EDNA. What did you do?

TOM. I told everyone I cheated. I was a hero. But I held on to my poetry book, bought some others. I keep them on this shelf. Haven't read one in years.

EDNA. Did you ever ask Lou?
TOM. To read me some poems?
EDNA. Yes.
TOM. Lou D'Marco makes a telephone bill sound worse than it is. Can you imagine what he'd do to Robert Browning?
EDNA. Aha.
TOM. Wordsworth. He's my favorite. Here's a guy who hung around, wrote poems about nature, rainbows, life, women ... (*From memory.*)
"She was a Phantom of delight
When first she gleamed upon my sight;
A lovely Apparition, sent
To be a moment's ornament;
Her eyes as stars of Twilight fair;
Like Twilight, too, her dusky hair;
But all things else about her drawn
From May-time and the cheerful Dawn;
A dancing Shape, an Image gay,
To haunt, to startle, and waylay.
A perfect Woman, nobly planned,
To warn, to comfort, and command;
And yet a Spirit still, and bright
With something of angelic light."
(*Then:*)
Could this guy write or what!
EDNA. Beautiful ...
TOM. His stuff is terrific.
EDNA. I never pictured you as someone who would like Shakespeare and Wordsworth, Thomas.

TOM. See? People build up these preconceived notions about people based on what? Nothing, really. Like I was watching this movie the other night ...

EDNA. Uh huh.

TOM. There was this blind guy and he's feeling some gal's face, and I guess it was all very tender and sensuous because there was all these violins.

EDNA. Yes.

TOM. And this guy, he's feeling away, and the gal, she's going, "Yes, John, please go ahead. Feel my face." And the guy's going, "I've been wondering what you look like for ever so long." He talked funny, you know, because he was British.

EDNA. Yes.

TOM. And this goes on for a while, I guess he's running his fingers all over her puss 'cause there's more and more violins every second. And he goes, he finally goes, "My word! You're beautiful!" Hah!

EDNA. Not true?

TOM. A total misconception.

EDNA. The girl's not beautiful?

TOM. No. I mean yeah, she's beautiful probably, but you can't tell what somebody looks like just feeling their face. You can't. *I* sure as hell can't. I can't tell if someone's ugly, beautiful or whatever. It's all baloney. "Blind people are these sensitive human beings that can paint pictures with their fingers." Wrong! I can barely tell my sister's face from a toaster! I don't have the slightest idea what anyone looks like if I feel their face. It's a total misconception created by Hollywood or some other bunch of assholes—excuse my French.

EDNA. Of course.

TOM. Okay, you can tell some absolute basics, like if someone is a hundred. They're going to have wrinkles. You can tell if someone's really old. Or if someone has a scar or an enormous nose, if they're bald ... something like that.

EDNA. Uh huh.

TOM. You can also tell if someone is really young. Their head is smaller. Aside from that, there's not much I can tell. There are a lot of notions about blind people that just aren't true. There's a lot they don't talk about. There's a lot they don't tell you. I'm starting to forget what certain things look like. My nephew, he's nine, I go to sit on my sister's couch and I feel something. I go, "Matty, is this your toy car?" The kid goes, "It's a bus." See, I was feeling it. I was holding it in my hand and I couldn't tell the difference between a car and a bus. I know they've both got four wheels, there's a lot of steel and glass, but as to the actual shape ... It's ... I can't really visualize that. What difference, huh? I'm not going to be driving either but still ... I used to know the difference between cars and buses. You know, I can't remember what I look like anymore. It started a few years ago. What I look like got a little fuzzy to me in my mind. Then it got worse. Now I try and picture what I look like and the picture comes out blank. When I shave I still do it in front of the mirror. I put my face before the mirror as though doing that will ... My own face has slipped away from me. I try ... I try to see myself but ... not anymore ...

EDNA. You have blue eyes.

TOM. What?

EDNA. Your eyes. They're blue. A light blue that looks almost grey in some light.

TOM. Are they cloudy?

EDNA. No.

TOM. They're not all white and milky?

EDNA. Not a bit.

TOM. For eight years I've wondered. Do my eyes stare in different places?

EDNA. No. They're normal.

TOM. Like a sighted person?

EDNA. Like a sighted person.

TOM. I've never asked Lou.

EDNA. It's not the kind of question one man can ask another.

TOM. I don't make eye contact with people.

EDNA. You come close.

TOM. But when I talk to you I don't look directly at you.

EDNA. Neither do a lot of sighted people. Your hair is blonde and baby fine.

TOM. Is it thinning?

EDNA. No. But you have some grey on the sides.

TOM. The old man. His had turned *white*.

EDNA. It makes you look distinguished.

TOM. Not old?

EDNA. No. Like a professor or a judge.

TOM. Yeah?

EDNA. Yes. Your skin is clear. A little on the pale side.

TOM. I don't go out enough.

EDNA. Your chin is round. You have high cheekbones. When you smile your eyes are little more than slits.

TOM. Yes.

EDNA. There's a small scar on your forehead.

TOM. I was ten. I got hit by a Coke bottle.

EDNA. You have long eyelashes for a man. They're quite beautiful. Your mouth is overwhelmingly kind. When you smile ...

TOM. Edna ...

EDNA. Yes, Tom?

TOM. I know we've only known each other for a week and you've probably got plans, tonight being New Year's Eve and all ...

EDNA. Yes?

TOM. It's not much but it's something I've done every New Year's Eve since I was a kid ...

EDNA. Yes.

TOM. We're just a couple blocks from Times Square. I usually bundle up good, take along a bottle of something to keep me warm ... I was wondering ...

EDNA. Yes, I'd love to.

TOM. Really?

EDNA. I think it would be wonderful to scream like madmen at midnight.

TOM. Well, all right ... Great ...

EDNA. Great ...

TOM. Yeah, great.

EDNA. Great.

(There is a moment where TOM would like to kiss Edna, however he has very little idea of how to approach it or if Edna is at all willing. EDNA wonders if she should help and initiate the kiss. The moment becomes more and more awkward, yet compelling. Just as it looks like this kiss might actually happen there is a KNOCK at the door.)

TOM. Who is it?
LOU. *(O.S.)* It's Lou.
TOM. Lou?
LOU. *(O.S.)* C'mon, open the door, it's fuckin' cold out here. I could piss ice cubes, I swear! C'mon, open up!

(TOM crosses to the door and unlocks it. LOU enters bundled well from the cold. HE carries a piece of luggage, a brown paper bag and a souvenir shopping bag from Vermont. HE also sports a warm looking hunter's hat—an obvious purchase from his trip.

During the following there is a certain air of insensitivity from LOU regarding the neatness of the apartment. His hat and gloves get tossed in different directions. When LOU misses the trash with the cap to a bottle of beer HE makes no effort to pick it up. This does not goes unnoticed by EDNA.)

LOU. Thanks, Tommy. Wow. Cold out there ... *(To Edna.)* Hiya ...
EDNA. Hello.
LOU. You know, I almost ... *(Registers apartment.)* Holy shit, what went on in here?!
TOM. *(Re: Edna.)* Hey, Lou, watch it with the language, huh?
LOU. Oh, yeah. Hey, I'm sorry. I been livin' with wolves for too long. Man, look at this place! I never seen it so clean.
EDNA. We tidied up a bit.

LOU. What'd you do? Use a rake? I've never seen this place look so good. (*Looking out window*.) Hey, you've got a fire escape! I never knew you had a fire escape!

TOM. What difference does it make?

LOU. It would make a *big* difference if there was a fire. (*Noticing the well-stocked cupboard*.) You got *food*. Lookit this. Eight, ten years I been comin' here, you ain't never had more than a can of tuna ... Look at all the food! And a dishcloth that matches a towel! Whooie!

TOM. I know you're having fun researching your article for *House and Garden* ... but don't you want to hustle on down to U-Haul, rent a truck and get out of town?

LOU. Yeah, well ...

EDNA. How was Vermont?

LOU. Cold and white. Here, Tom, I got you some maple syrup. I wish I could tell you I bought it at some folksy little place from an old geezer with a pipe and suspenders, but I didn't. I bought it at a souvenir store when the bus stopped at the Nelson E. Rockefeller Memorial Rest Oasis.

TOM. You took the bus back?

LOU. Yeah.

TOM. I thought you were driving up with Mona.

LOU. Drove up—took the bus back.

TOM. Uh oh.

EDNA. Something go wrong?

LOU. I'm not movin' to Vermont, Tommy. I'm not movin' nowhere.

TOM. You're not?

LOU. I'm back to stay.

TOM. Hey, all right!!!

(TOM and LOU engage in some macho hugging, back slapping and boxing. EDNA manages a weak smile.)

TOM. That's terrific, man! What happened?

LOU. Aw ... I had the Christmas from Hell. You're talkin' to a very depressed and disillusioned person. Mona comes to pick me up and the first thing I realize is she drives a Citroen. You know this car? Lays low to the ground until you start it—then the whole thing lifts up like a vacuum cleaner.

TOM. So?

LOU. So it's the stupidest car ever made. If schmucks had an official car it would be a Citroen. I shoulda known right then. I should never of gotten into that car. We get to Mona's parents house and the first person I meet is Mona's sister Jane. "Jane has an alternate lifestyle," Mona's been tellin' me. "Jane has an alternate lifestyle." I figured that means she's a vegetarian or she hang glides or somethin'. Jane turns out to be a lesbian. I mean a *veteran* lesbian. A confirmed, dedicated, card-carrying, short haircut, khaki pants with heavy-duty work shoes lesbian! And Jane's brought her "friend" Bobby. Actually it's Roberta, but nobody's called her that since Eisenhower was President. Then I meet Mona's father. "He was blacklisted," Mona's been tellin' me. Like it was some honor. Fine, he was blacklisted. I never had the nerve to ask, "Blacklisted from *what*?" I just kept my mouth shut and looked impressed. Mona's mother comes in the room and her folks begin the Christmas Eve "festivities." Her father goes, he goes, "Mona, Jane ... your mother and I are getting a divorce." Holy mackerel. Did it hit the fan! What went on for the next five hours! There's no way to describe how tense and nervous and weird and painful everything was. If it had been my family, someone woulda got a gun and killed everyone. At least it woulda been over quick. Not Mona's family. They believe in squeezing out every drop of suffering and agony through *talking*. Mona takes her father into the den, Jane-the-lesbian takes Mom in the kitchen. There's wailin' and cryin'. You hear bits of stuff being said. "She never forgave me!" "His work has been his wife!" "I can't take it anymore." Mona's ex-husband Burton drops by. Burton is dropping off their kid. He's twelve. Weird, sick looking little weasel who takes forty different pills a day for all the stuff that's wrong with 'im. Mona can't wait to spread the joy. "Sweetheart, grandma and grandpa are getting divorced!" The kid goes into an asthma attack like I never seen! People are screamin' an' cryin', "You did this! This is your fault! Call an ambulance! No, don't!" You know, the TV was on through all this. Here these two old farts are ending a marriage of fifty years on Christmas Eve and there's Andy Williams singin' "Holy Night" from Hawaii. Mona's ex hasn't left. He just keeps goin', "Anything I can do?" Finally, Mona takes me aside and says, "Lou, Burton and I are going out for coffee." I spent my Christmas Eve playin' checkers with Bobby-the-lesbo listening to two old communists cry upstairs. We played maybe ten games in a row, didn't speak a word, either one of us. Gets to be one in the mornin'. All you can hear is the sound of the clock tickin' and the wind outside. Me an' Bobby ain't said a word for hours, and all of a sudden Bobby looks up at me an' says ... she says, "You know, Lou, I'm a lesbian." And I've got to be polite and act *surprised*. Go, "Really?" When all I really want to say is, "Oh, I just thought you *liked* looking like Ernest

Borgnine!" Or, "Let's go look under the tree. Maybe Santa's left you a vibrator!" That was my Christmas in Vermont. I didn't go skiin'. I didn't go tobogganin', or talk with colorful old guys spinnin' yarns. Mona an' me did *not* look for a house to rent or jobs to get. That plan was abandoned instantly. It was just a stupid pipe dream. I was lookin' to change my life, Tom. (*Partially to Edna.*) I was lookin' to make myself into somebody new, somebody different. Guys like us, Tom ... from this neighborhood, from our backgrounds ... nothing changes for us. They don't make miracles in Hell's Kitchen.

EDNA. You'll meet someone else.

LOU. Where? Where's a guy like me goin' to meet a woman at my age, huh? I work five days a week, ten, twelve hours a day at the Terminal Bar and Grill.

EDNA. Women go to taverns.

LOU. Hey, Tom. You hear that? "Women go to taverns."

TOM. Don't make fun. She hasn't seen much of life.

LOU. Edna, the women who crawl into the Terminal Bar and Grill are on the food chain right next to Dobermans.

EDNA. Oh ...

TOM. But in any case, you're back to stay, huh?

LOU. I ain't never settin' foot outta Manhattan again.

TOM. All right!

LOU. Yeah.

(*TOM and LOU "high five."*)

LOU. Hey, Tom, know what I seen?
TOM. What?

LOU. The cops, they were settin' up barriers on Times Square. Gettin' ready for tonight.

TOM. You think the weather's going to cut down the size of the crowd?

LOU. Who cares! We're gonna be screamin' our lungs out! Ahooo!

TOM. (*Matching Lou.*) Ahooo!

EDNA. You know ...

LOU. (*Interrupting.*) Ahooo! Hey, look, Tommy. Check out what I got. (*LOU rummages through his brown paper bag. HE whips out an air horn and gives it a blast.*)

TOM. All right!

LOU. You believe it?

TOM. Man, that thing is *loud*!

LOU. Gotta be careful with it. Don't hold it next to your ear.

TOM. That's all I need. To be blind *and* deaf.

(THEY laugh.)

TOM. What else you get?

LOU. I got all kinds o' shit. Noise makers, hats ... (*LOU takes other New Year's Eve items out of his brown paper bag; hats, horns, noise makers, etc.*)

TOM. Where'd you get all this?

EDNA. Thomas ...

LOU. (*Interrupts.*) Some guy down the street. He's sellin' everything.

TOM. He have any cherry bombs?

LOU. Naw, but I got some at my place from last year.

EDNA. Tom ...

TOM. Terrific.

EDNA. Tom.

TOM. (*To Edna.*) Just a sec. (*To Lou.*) Wouldn't be a New Year's Eve without cherry bombs. (*To Edna.*) Yeah?

EDNA. Have you forgotten?

TOM. Huh? Oh! Yeah, right. Sorry. Lou, Edna's comin'.

LOU. She's what?

TOM. She's coming with us. I invited her to Times Square.

LOU. Oh. (*Operating noise maker.*) Hey, Tom, you like this one?

TOM. It's nice but it's nothing like that air horn.

LOU. Naw, this baby's a beaut!

(LOU goes to blast the air horn again but Edna stops him.)

EDNA. Please!

(LOU puts the air horn down.)

EDNA. Thank you.

LOU. Sorry. It's just that we get so excited over New Year's Eve.

TOM. Man, this is great. I got Edna here to read to me, you're back from this stupid Vermont thing ... Hey! We gotta celebrate.

LOU. Huh?

TOM. I don't want to wait 'til tonight. We oughta have a toast right now.

LOU. Sure. You got a bottle in the house?

EDNA. There's some whiskey.

TOM. (*Getting his coat.*) Naw naw ... not that. Champagne! We've got to toast the New Year with champagne! Nothing less will do. Lou's my oldest friend. Edna, you're my newest friend. If that's not a celebration I don't know what is! Let me run out to the liquor store. They always got some champagne that's cold.

LOU. Want me to get it, Tom?

TOM. Lou, I've got to do more for myself. Know what I mean? Stay here. I'll be right back. And hey. Don't go putting any moves on my date for New Year's Eve, huh?

(*TOM laughs. LOU and EDNA respond with nervous laughs. TOM exits. There is an uncomfortable silence, finally:*)

EDNA. So ...
LOU. So.

(*There is another uncomfortable silence. Finally:*)

LOU. You did good.

EDNA. With what?

LOU. With what. With him. With Tom. With his apartment. You did good.

EDNA. Oh. We just tidied up a little.

LOU. No, you did a lot more than "tidy." You did good. I never liked how filthy it was in here. Christ, I tried everything. Teasing, shaming ... everything. There were times I just wanted to take a bucket with hot water and Lysol and ... looks like that's just what you done.

EDNA. Once we got started, it was easy.

LOU. I guess what the place needed was a woman's touch. I mean look what I got done in eight years and look what you done in eight days.

EDNA. We didn't do that much.

LOU. Sure. You, uh ... come by here what time generally?

EDNA. Generally?

LOU. Yeah, generally.

EDNA. About ten in the morning. Maybe eleven.

LOU. Ten.

EDNA. Maybe eleven.

LOU. And you stay 'til when?

EDNA. It depends.

LOU. You stay 'til ...

EDNA. Four, five.

LOU. All day.

EDNA. Well, not *all* day. Well, yes.

LOU. And what is that, two days a week? Three?

EDNA. We haven't worked out an exact schedule ...

LOU. How many days a week?

EDNA. It's only been one week so far. We haven't formalized any ...

LOU. How many days a week?

EDNA. Tom and I haven't ...

LOU. How many ...

EDNA. Seven! Every. Day. So far, that is. I've been here every ... all eight days. There seems to be a lot to do.

LOU. You love 'im?

EDNA. What!

LOU. You love 'im? Are you in love with Tom?

EDNA. I don't see how that's any of your concern.

LOU. He's my best friend.

EDNA. Congratulations.

LOU. He's blind as a bat. I've been lookin' out for 'im almost nine years. He meets a new chick—I ask.

EDNA. And how many "new chicks" has he met in nine years? I guess they file up here on a regular basis. You perform this service often, do you?

LOU. You ... never mind. Do you love Tom?

EDNA. Did you love Mona?

LOU. Seems to me you do.

EDNA. Just stop it.

LOU. If you didn't love 'im, you'd be denyin' it left an' right.

EDNA. Stop it!

LOU. One thing people don't want to be accused of is lovin' someone they don't.

EDNA. It's none of your concern.

LOU. Right. It's none of my concern that you're in love with Tom.

EDNA. You're going to tell him.

LOU. Tell "him?"

EDNA. Tom ... You're going to tell him.

LOU. Tell him what?

EDNA. Everything! You're going to tell him everything! About me, about ... everything.

LOU. What "everything"?

EDNA. Stop it! Stop toying with me! You're going to tell him, aren't you?!

LOU. He's my best friend. Besides, he's gonna ask me. The second me an' him is alone he's gonna ask me as sure as Christmas, "Hey, Lou. What's Edna look like?"

EDNA. And you're going to tell him.

LOU. He's my best friend.

EDNA. You're going to tell him. Your way. The way men have. That cruel, common way they talk sometimes. That awful way of talking that men think makes them more manly or weary or something. "Tom, I'm sorry I gotta be the one, but this Edna chick is a dog, pal. And there's something wrong with her leg or her hand or something." Won't you feel good then!

LOU. Hey, look, first of all, I'm not gonna tell Tom in no crude manner like you just said. I'll tell 'im with respect. Trust me. If he asks me, I'll tell 'im you don't look good in a *nice* way. Second of all, if I don't tell him he would just find out anyway.

EDNA. No. That's just it. He wouldn't find out. Not really. Not in the way he'd find out from you.

LOU. You're crazy.

EDNA. In his mind he's built a much kinder image of me. I'm not saying he thinks I'm beautiful, but he sees me as someone special. I know he does.

LOU. Yeah, well ...

EDNA. And if you came back six months from now or six weeks from now or even six *days* from now and you were to tell Tom anything negative about me ...

LOU. Yeah?

EDNA. He wouldn't believe you.

LOU. Why?

EDNA. Because he'd be in love with me. You could say whatever you'd like and he wouldn't believe you. He *couldn't* believe you.

LOU. No way.

EDNA. It's what falling in love does to a person. Have you ever seen a couple in their forties or fifties that's obviously been together for many years?

LOU. Huh?

EDNA. And let's say the woman is still quite attractive but the man has simply let himself go. He's overweight, his belly hangs over his pants, his face is puffy, he's lost his hair, he needs a few trips to the dentist.

LOU. So?

EDNA. So—do you think he looked like that when his wife met him?

LOU. What?

EDNA. Do you think they were in college and she said to herself, "Wow, look at the fat, sloppy guy with bad teeth and no hair!"?

LOU. Some guys just get like that.

EDNA. Of course! He was probably handsome once.

LOU. So?

EDNA. So if the woman is still attractive, why does she put up with a man who looks like that?

LOU. How the fuck should I know!?

EDNA. It's because she doesn't see it! Not what we see. Not all of it. When she looks at him she sees the handsome man she fell in love with. When we fall in love with someone there's a moment when we take a picture of that person, an emotional snapshot, that we carry with us forever. If we're lucky, if we're very, very lucky, the person we fall in love with will always resemble that snapshot.

LOU. What are you talking about?

EDNA. I'm talking about loving someone. Thomas is getting ready to fall in love with me. He hasn't felt like he's worth doing that in a very long time but his self respect is ... well, you saw him. He's different now. Thomas is changing. We'll be in Times Square tonight.

We'll both be drinking. He'll kiss me at midnight and sketch a picture in his mind that will last him a lifetime. Nothing will change it. Not even if you wait a day to tell him what you think is so important. I've never been surer of anything. When my father first took my mother out, they went to Coney Island. They rode the carousel six times in a row. They went on some other rides, the Ferris wheel, I believe, the wild mouse ... My father bought my mother a bag of peanuts. He tipped the man selling them an extra nickel and she thought he was "devilishly mad" seeing as how it was the height of the Depression. Then my mother didn't feel too well, probably one of the rides. They sat on a bench on the boardwalk. My father listened to every word my mother said that night as though she were the most intelligent, fascinating woman he had ever met. More than that he thought she was funny. Yes. She made him laugh. It made her feel very special. To make a person feel they are bright is one thing. But to make them feel they are witty and clever ... They spent the rest of their night sitting on that bench talking. My mother has shown me the bench. I've been to "the bench." The lights danced behind them, music blared from the rides, and in the middle of all that, when the moment was absolutely right, my mother took a snapshot of my father with her heart. She fell in love and this was the man and the moment she would remember until the day she dies. She tucked away her photo in her soul. As the years went by, my father ceased to find my mother funny. He also did not find her interesting or intelligent or any of the other things he found her to be that night. Worse than that, he has let her know it. With every disinterested look, with every silent goodbye. Was it last week or the week before ...? I'm not sure but my father was on his way out and my mother, what's *left* of my mother, came shuffling by and he took one end of his scarf and tossed it over his shoulder and, I suppose, for the briefest moment, he resembled something called dashing to a woman like my mother who still listens to big band music, and he said to my mother, "Adios, sweetie!" and the old woman's eyes filled with colored lights and cotton candy! You could almost hear a calliope playing in the background. Her face! Her expression! The life that flared up in her! "There! That's him! The kind and gentle man who loves me!" She forgave *everything*! He was the handsome young man on the bench again. It was only for a second but a second was all it took. It didn't make my mother's day—it made her *life!* Don't you see? You don't love someone for who they are. You love someone for who you *think* they are. If Tom thinks I'm pretty what right do you have to take that away from him? What am I going to do with the picture I took of Tom? What will I do with my picture?! He stood there and recited a poem for me. A poem he memorized in high school. Wearing his favorite Christmas sweater. The one he thinks is red and white. You saw him! Running out to buy champagne ... What am I to do with my picture? Why would you think ...

(EDNA cannot continue. Neither SHE nor LOU can speak for several beats. Finally the door opens and TOM is standing there. HE is speaking to someone down the hall.)

TOM. Listen, that's a cute pooch. What's his name? Diablo? I love it! *(Pause.)* He's a dog! Sometimes he can't help himself. Hey, Diablo ... Happy New Year, fella. You, too. Hey, Feliz Navidad! (*TOM enters. HE carries a bag and happily goes about the task of serving champagne for three.*) Nice guy down the hall. Turns out he's not Puerto Rican. He's from El Salvador. Man, it is *cold* outside. Must be ten, twelve degrees. Get this, I ran into Herman the German at the liquor store. Lou, you know Herman. Sees me buying champagne and has the nerve to say to me, "Wadda *you* celebratin'?" As though I've got nothin' to celebrate. The *nerve* on that guy. "Wadda *you* celebratin'?" I looked him straight in the eye—well, I *hope* I looked him straight in the eye—I said, "Herman, I'm going home to celebrate the fact that I don't have to stand here and smell your *breath* anymore. Waddaya do every morning? Gargle with *shit*?" Excuse my French. Man, I would've given anything to see the look on his Nazi puss. Here's a guy, stinks like shit his whole life, has no friends at all and has never, *ever* bought me a drink. Has the gall to say to me on the morning of New Year's Eve, "What are *you* celebratin'?" Germans! Why does the word "charming" *not* come to mind? Lou, you want the glass with Fred or Barney? I can tell which is which, you know. Fred has more paint on the glass. Lou, you usually like Fred, huh?

LOU. Sure.

TOM. Then you get Fred. Edna, you get Pebbles and Bamm Bamm, because it's the only girl glass I got.

(*There is a moment when neither LOU nor EDNA know what to say. The silence seems to go on forever. Finally:*)

LOU. She's not here.

TOM. What?

LOU. Edna. She went down the hallway to the can. You know, had to powder her nose.

TOM. Well, thanks for tellin' me. Christ, I'm talking away here like she's in the room.

LOU. Sorry.

TOM. Is she okay?

LOU. Yeah, she's fine. Just had to go to the little girl's room. And not a minute too soon.

TOM. Huh?

LOU. Edna. She didn't get out of here a minute too soon, Tommy.

TOM. What are you talking?

LOU. Leave me alone like that with her. Here, in your place. Don't do that again.

TOM. Huh?

LOU. I'm your best friend so don't go leavin' Edna with me no more.

TOM. Why?

LOU. Why! Because I'm only human is why. The chick is fuckin' gorgeous. A couple more minutes I woulda been hittin' on her for myself.

TOM. Hey, hey ... watch it. Edna's spoken for. Lay the fuck off.

LOU. Well, don't leave her with me like that no more.

TOM. Just keep it in your pants, D'Marco. Understand?

LOU. I understand.

TOM. All right.

LOU. All right.

TOM. She really pretty?

LOU. Trust me. This chick is a fox.

TOM. I had a feeling. You know, when you lose your sense of sight, your other senses sharpen. The way she sounds, the way she moves, little things, the way she picks things up, puts them down, always real lady like ... feminine. Sexy. And the way she smells, not all perfumey, but nice, you know? She walks by and for half a moment she's still there. It starts to drive you crazy.

LOU. Yeah.

TOM. I had a feeling she was someone special.

LOU. I'd better duck outta Times Square tonight, Tom. Three's a crowd, huh?

TOM. Thanks, Lou.

(EDNA opens the door to the apartment, then closes it, pretending she has returned from her trip to the bathroom. Her voice quivers with emotion.)

EDNA. Oh, Tom. You're back. That was quick.

TOM. When it comes to toasting the New Year, I don't mess around.

EDNA. You certainly don't.

TOM. You okay? Something wrong?

EDNA. I'm just very cold all of a sudden. It's so chilly in the hallway.

TOM. *(Re: champagne.)* Well, this'll get your fire burning.

LOU. Yeah, let's drink up. I still gotta unpack.

(THEY each take a glass.)

TOM. Lou, you got any wishes for the New Year?

LOU. No.

EDNA. There must be something.
TOM. Yeah, you're always complaining.
EDNA. Don't you wish for anything?
LOU. I just wish I never see Vermont again.
TOM. A lovely wish, Lou.
LOU. You got a wish, Tommy?
TOM. I wish that the three of us can become good friends.
EDNA. That was going to be my wish.
LOU. Good, we all got a wish, I'm so happy, bottoms up.
TOM. Happy New Year.

(THEY all drink.)

LOU. Nice stuff, Tom. What is it?
TOM. *(Joking.)* Dom Perignon. Ninety bucks a bottle.
LOU. *(Playing along.)* Really? The label don't say "Dom Perignon."
TOM. What *does* it say?
LOU. "Larry's."
TOM. That darn salesman!

(TOM, LOU and EDNA laugh.)

LOU. See ya later, ya potato head, ya.
TOM. Get out of here, you dumb Italian. Happy New Year.
EDNA. Goodbye, Lou. *(EDNA gives Lou a long, heartfelt hug.)*
LOU. Happy New Year ... *(LOU exits.)*
TOM. Good guy ... a real friend.

EDNA. Yes, he is. To real friends.
TOM. You got it.

(THEY drink.)

TOM. By the way, Lou can't make it tonight.
EDNA. Oh?
TOM. Something he had to do. No big deal. You and I will just have to pick up the slack. Make the noise of three people.
EDNA. And we will!
TOM. Ahoooo!
EDNA. (*Mildly.*) Who-ray!
TOM. It needs work. Wait a minute! Is this your first New Year's in Times Square?
EDNA. Yes.
TOM. Then we've got to preserve this event for posterity. (*TOM feels around the kitchen table for the items Lou brought with him.*) Where's that stuff Lou brought?
EDNA. Here. What are you ...?
TOM. I got it. Here they are. (*TOM finds two silly party hats. HE puts one on himself and gives the other to EDNA.*)
EDNA. What are these for?
TOM. For New Year's Eve! (*TOM goes about the task of retrieving his camera from where it hangs on the wall and making space on a shelf that is eye level.*)
EDNA. What are you doing?
TOM. I'm going to take a picture.
EDNA. But how ... I don't feel like having my picture taken.

TOM. Uh uh. We've *got* to do this. It's a *sin* if we don't. That's what Sister Mary Dominick taught us at Our Lady of Perpetual Pain, Suffering and Agony. (*TOM hands the camera to EDNA.*) See the red ring on the lens. The f-stop ... What's it on?

EDNA. Two point five ...

TOM. Perfect. Now focus on the shelf.

EDNA. Hmm?

TOM. Focus on the shelf. You'll see. Move this part here. See? (*TOM helps EDNA with focusing the camera.*) Look through here, move this like so to focus ...

EDNA. I see. Yes. Wait. Hold on ...

TOM. This is great. I'm inventing blind photography.

EDNA. There. I think that's it.

TOM. Now, don't move.

EDNA. But ...

TOM. Don't move. (*TOM crosses to the shelf and puts the camera on it. HE points it toward Edna.*) Is it pointing at you?

EDNA. No, I ... it's ...

TOM. To the left?

EDNA. Yes, a little.

TOM. (*Moves the camera.*) Like so?

EDNA. A little more. Tom, you can't expect to ...

TOM. Is that it?

EDNA. Yes. It's pointing at me. I guess.

TOM. Got your hat on?

EDNA. Yes.

TOM. Get ready.

EDNA. You're not actually going to ...

TOM. You bet I am!

(TOM presses the timer device on the camera. HE races over to join Edna. THEY stand side by side wearing their party hats, holding their drinks.)

    EDNA. This is silly.
    TOM. Yes, it is, isn't it?! Thank you! You're welcome!

(EDNA giggles.)

    TOM. Edna?
    EDNA. Yes, Tom?
    TOM. Happy New Year.
    EDNA. Happy New Year.

(THEY smile at each other and the camera takes its picture. The LIGHTS fade to BLACK.)

THE END

COSTUME PLOT

EDNA
ACT I
Navy cotton tights
Gold turtleneck
Paisley pleated skirt
Cranberry cotton sweater
Gold hoop earrings
Watch w/leather band
Black boots
Navy wool coat
Green/maroon paisley scarf
Black leather gloves
Black leather purse
ACT II
Remove: purse, gloves, earrings, coat, scarf, boots, sweater, skirt, turtleneck, tights
Add:
Hose
Blue floral dress
Blue pumps
Pearl drop earrings
Coat (same)
Scarf (same)
Gloves (same)
Purse (same)

LOU
ACT I
White T-shirt
Grey waffle weave pullover

Levi jeans w/belt
Green plaid cotton shirt
Brown socks
Black leather boots
Grey stocking cap
Brown leather jacket
Black half-glasses

ACT II

Remove: jacket, boots, shirt, jeans, cap, glasses
Add:
Blue wool plaid shirt
Brown corduroy pants
"Sorrel" boots
Grey muffler
Red/black plaid hunter's cap
Brown leather jacket (same)
Brown knit/leather gloves

TOM

ACT I

"Dirty" T-shirt
Blue plaid shirt (added on stage)
Blue plaid pants
Dark grey socks
Dark brown socks
Maroon corduroy slippers

ACT II

Remove: slippers, socks, shirt, pants, T-shirt
Add:
White T-shirt
Blue dress shirt w/orange stripes
Grey/brown polo pants

Dark brown dress socks
"The" sweater
Maroon slip-on dress shoes
Tan corduroy coat
Grey fedora

PROPERTY PLOT

Desk
Desk chair
Shelves
Radiator
Bath tub
Stove
Fridge
Sink (in counter unit) w/practical water
Cabinet
Book shelf
Dresser
Bed
Center table
Chairs
Desk lamp – practical
Wall sconce – practical (light bulb needs to unscrew)
Hanging light fixtures – practical (light bulb needs to unscrew)
Television
Small radio
Dirty dishes in sink
Garbage
Pieces of clothing
35mm camera (1975)
Books
Black & white photos (see script for description)
Jelly jar glasses
Whiskey bottle
Record player
Records

Safety chain for front door
Coins
Mail (brought on by Lou and as dressing in bath tub)
Christmas card
Checkbook
Deposit slips
Disability checks
Pamphlet from blind office
Stapler
Money: 20's, 10's, 5's, 1's
Empty beer bottle
Trash can
Broom (rigged to break)
Gift-wrapped bottle of scotch
Glasses
Can of chili
Dead paint
Light bulb package
Beer bottles
Pens, pencils
Photo supply stuff
Dish towel
Trash cans by desk and in kitchen
Apple
ACT II
Healthy plant
Water kettle
Tea pot
Tea
Tea cups
Piece of luggage
Brown bag with air horn

Souvenir shopping bag from Vermont w/maple syrup
Party hats, horns, noise makers
Brown bag
Bottle of champagne
Glasses
Blind folding walking stick
New broom
Newspapers, book and magazines
Phone preset on desk
Sugar bowl
Spoons
Dish drainer
Crackers in a cracker tin
Small plate for crackers
Metal mop bucket
Paper napkins

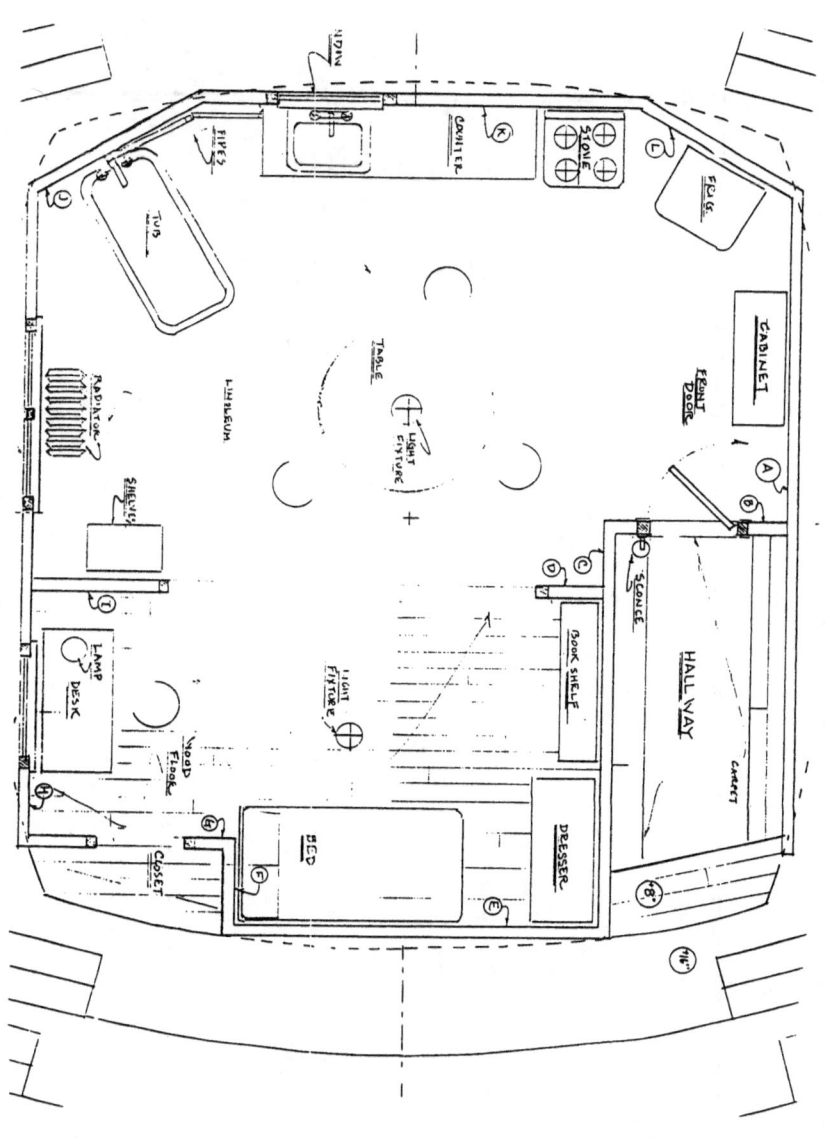

Also By

Jim Geoghan

ONLY KIDDING

OTHER TITLES AVAILABLE FROM SAMUEL FRENCH

THREE YEARS FROM "THIRTY"
Mike O'Malley

Comic Drama / 4m, 3f / Unit set
This funny, poignant story of a group of 27-year-olds who have known each other since college sold out during its limited run at New York City's Sanford Meisner Theater. Jessica Titus, a frustrated actress living in Boston, has become distraught over local job opportunities and she is feeling trapped in her long standing relationship with her boyfriend Tom. She suddenly decides to pursue her dreams in New York City. Unbeknownst to her, Tom plans to propose on the evening she has chosen to leave him. The ensuing conflict ripples through their lives and the lives of their roommates and friends, leaving all of them to reconsider their careers, the paths of their souls and the questions, demands and definition of commitment.

SAMUELFRENCH.COM

www.ingramcontent.com/pod-product-compliance
Lightning Source LLC
Chambersburg PA
CBHW070646300426
44111CB00013B/2297